# Literary Cats

British Library Cataloguing in Publication Data
A record for this book is available from the British Library

ISBN 0 340 86396X

Design by Janette Revill

Printed in China

Hodder & Stoughton
A Division of Hodder Headline Ltd
338 Euston Road
London NW1 3BH
www.madaboutbooks.com

# Literary Cats

# HEATHER HACKING

HODDER &
STOUGHTON

# PERCY HYSSE SHELLEY

T'HE FLAMBOYANT POET was in constant competition with his playmate, George Byron, as to who could be the most outrageous. For added piquancy, Percy Hysse was married to Hairy Shelley, the author of *Frankenstein*. So which 'beasty boy' did she choose as a model for the monster? Perce *has* to be odds on favourite: he wrote:

*My name is Fuzzymandias, King of Cats:*
*Look upon my claws, ye Mouses, and despair.*

*Percy and George on*
*holiday in Ibiza*

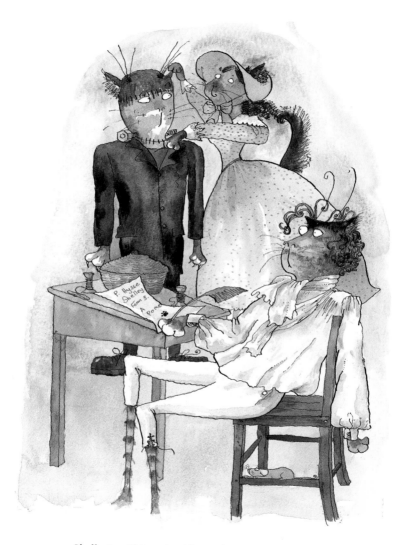

*Shelley's wife's embroidery takes a sinister turn*

*Fluff and Birdsnest on the Riviera*

# FLUFF SCOTT FITZGERALD

*I*N THE WILD 1920s and 30s Fluff and his friend, the unkempt, over-furry writer, Birdsnest Hemingway, lapped up cream cocktails and snorted catnip together, caterwauling all night on roof tops from New York to Antibes. This riotous life was mirrored in Fitzgerald's hedonistic novel, *The Great Catsby*. Their habit of experimenting with zany things to eat inspired *Tender is the Newt*. Its sequel: *Pterrible is the Pterodactyl* has been lost.

*The Charleston – a popular dance of the 'The Great Catsby' era*

*Barbie and her favourite lapdog*

# BARBARA CATLAND

This gorgeous white Persian regularly employed a couple of spiders to perch on her eyelids to imitate thick black lashes. Barbie banned understatement from her lifestyle by whirling from cocktail party to debutantes' ball in a haze of pink tulle and puffs of *Eau d'Haddock* perfume. Her hundreds of romantic novels included such breathless titles as *The Princess and the Paw-Paw*; *A Prawn in Love*; *A Hazard of Herrings*; *Love for Limpets* and *The Capricious Canapé*.

*A tender moment from
'The Prince and the Paw-Paw'*

*Leo emerges with chapter 1*

# LEO TOLSTOY

TOLSTOY COULD NOT write a short book to save his life. His wife begged him to write a short story to get some food on the table quickly. His answer was to lock himself in the garden shed for five years and emerge with the doorstopper, *Fur and Peace*. It took him another year to decide if it should be *Purr and Plaice*, *Fur and Meece*, *Claw and Teeth* or set it to music and call it *Napoleon on Ice*.

*Leo wore out many proof-readers*

FUR and PEACE?

Alf Furred and the lovely
Tabby of Shalott

# ALF FURRED, LORD TENNYSON

## 'THE TABBY OF SHALOTT'

*On either side the river lie*
*Long fields of barley and of rye,*
*That hide the mice but fool not I;*
*Who thro' the field goes slinking by*
*To where I will Catch-a-lot;*
*And up and down the mice will go,*
*Fleeing where the lilies blow*
*Straight into my jaws below.*
*That's yer lot!*

The Tabby of Shallot lolloping
around with lilies

*Purrthos playfully parries the* petite *author*

# ALEXANDRE DORMOUSE

*N*O ONE COULD write such thigh-slapping, swashbuckling, heart-stopping adventures as Dormouse. His fabulously famous *The Three Mousequetières* introduced the world to the lightning-swift swordplay of Purrthos, Hairthos, Arameece and Dog'tagnan. His devilishly vengeful *The Cat of Monte Cristo* demonstrated the fury of a cat that someone had dared to lock in a castle with no catflap.

*The Cat in the Iron Mouse*

# FURGINIA WOLF

*F*URGINIA WAS A snob from the tip of her flared nostrils to the point of her arrogantly swishing tail. Her high-handed putdowns bristled the neck fur on many an insulted artist or writer. She was not bothered: a lack of concern which emerges in her short novel '*Who's Afraid of Me?*' Other works include *To the Lighthouse* (for cats whose mad half hour includes running up and down stairs in spirals) and *Orlando – The Marmalade Cat.*

*Furginia detects the faint whiff of peasant*

*Mrs Wolf giving one the once over*

# SAMMY TAIL COLERIDGE

*H*ERE IS THE pie-eyed poet puffing 'Devon Dandelion' and writing 'Xanadu'. His creative trips depended on what he had had for supper ('The Ancient Mariner' followed a sprat and gherkin pie).

> *In Xanadu did Khubla Khat*
> *A stately pleasure home decree*
> *Where Alf the sacred river ran*
> *Through caverns measureless to man*
> *Down to a sunless sea.*

Sammy was confused. 'Alf' was his valet, Alf Watts, who ran down to 'The Cavern' in Burnham-on-Sea to pick up his master's snorting dust.

Powdered Dandelion

*Sammy enjoying an evening in*

# VICTOR HUGE

*H*ERE IS THE giant French novelist, huge in every way. His weighty novels had massive sales and his generous waistline increased with his fame and wealth. Victor liked to write about food and his best-known work, *The Lunchpack of Notre Dame*, reflects his passion. The bell ringer, Quasimodo, alights on a parapet of Notre Dame Cathedral with a takeaway. His mission is to save the skinny gypsy, Esmeralda, from a life as a stick insect impersonator.

*Victor and Mrs Huge watch his 'Les Miserables' on TV*

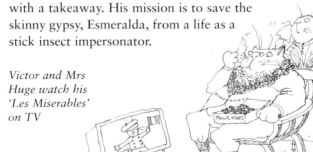

*Quasimodo's picnic on a parapet*

# PAWS CHRISTIAN ANDERSEN

*H*ow COPENHAGEN'S MOST famous son ever escaped the embrace of the straitjacket is a mystery. Depressed, demented and fidgety as a bottle of wasps, he turned to writing fairy tales for children as an emotional outlet. These macabre masterpieces include *The Little Mermaid* – this revealed that Andersen's ideal woman was half herring. His tales, which out-grimmed the Brothers Grimm by several whiskers, began the trend for children to sleep with the light on.

*Danish children had trouble sleeping*

*Paws with his Little Mermaid and Ugly Duckling*

*The Catterbury Pilgrims swap recipes*

# GEOFFURRY CHAUCER

CHAUCER'S *Catterbury Tails* tells of several celebrity chefs making a trip to the famous Thomas à Bucket o'Nuggets cookery school in Kent. To pass the time, they swap recipes on the way: 'Lampreys in Limpet Sauce' (from the Fishwife of Bath); 'Snippets of Snipe' (the Spin Doctor's Tail); 'Vole Roll: a Pancake for Shrew Tuesday' (the Priest's Tail) and 'Peacock and pea Pavlova with a Pease parfait' (the Pea Marketing Board)

*Peacock Pavlova followed by Knotted Eel en gelée*

# THE GRUNTË SISTERS

*T*HREE LITERARY TALENTS with gigantic egos packed into one tiny parsonage was bound to produce the odd spat; but *these* ladies, who had already bumped off their brother for being untalented and a *boy*, could have tantrums that the Brothers Karamazov could only dream about. These were followed by a winter of sulking, a month growling under a blanket and an hour of hissing like sugar burning on a black lead stove. Charlotte wrote *Jane Airhead*, based on Anne; Anne wrote *The Tyrant of Wildcat Hall*, about Charlotte, and Emily's *Withering Slights* was a catalogue of sisterly criticism. After publication day a cloud of cat fur hung over ten acres of moorland.

'Withering Slights':
*Cathy and Heathcliffe*

*A typical truce at Haworth Parsonage*

*The Brownears and their dog, Flush*

# ELIZABETH AND ROBPURRED BROWNEAR

W HEN THE HANDSOME brown tortoiseshell poet, Robpurred Brownear, fell in love with the poetess, Elizabeth Barrett, a veritable poetry festival ensued as they wrote sonnets together about their mutual passion, Portuguese sardines. They eloped to Italy to enjoy marriage and to have capricious fun making 'calamari' rhyme with 'Ferrari'.

# EVELYN PAUGH

*T*HIS SQUASHED-FACE Persian had a temperament to match his sour expression. His masterpiece, *Codshead Regurgitated*, is an acidic view of the lives of aristocratic show cats. During the over-fishing prohibitions of the cod war years, Charles discovers that his upper-crust friend, Sebastian, *and* his beloved teddy bear, are addicted to quantities of seafood. In the mausoleum of the Yorkshire family mansion, 'Codshead', Charles finds the tell-tale stash of fish bones and a trawler licence.

*Paugh in one of his happier moods*

*Charles finds Sebastian's guilty secret*

*Marlowe and his wardrobe gurus*

# CHRISTOFUR (KIT) MARLOWE

*A* CONTEMPORARY OF WILLIAM SHAKESPURR, Kit had many identities; as a spy, a wit, a dandy, poet and playwright. He wrote *Dr Fur-Truss* about a cat who sold his Dover Sole to the devil in order to buy a corset that would allow him to fit into his tight but devilishly-fashionable doublet. In this portrait, the gorgeous Marlowe (as Fur-Truss) is being advised by good and evil angels on the pros and cons of sole sales.

*Kit at his tailors*

# ISABELLA, MRS BEETON

WRITTEN IN VICTORIAN times, Mrs Beeton's cookbook *One Hundred Ways with a Rat* still remains the gold standard. Her ingenious and thrifty recipes include: Rat-tail Ratatouille, Ratafia biscuits, Arrowrat biscuits and Mouse Mousse.

Recipe for Rat-tail Ratatouille:
*Take 60 rat tails. Marinate for 24 hours in Gentlemen's Relish. Throw on barbeque. Drizzle with cream.* Excellent with a *Mouse-on Rothschild* '68.

*Mrs Beeton makes her fine tira-mousu*

*Mrs Beeton and her* ratatouille *recipe*

# 'SILKIE' COLLINS

GLORIOUSLY SMOOTH, SILKY and exquisitely groomed, Silkie took a ghastly fright walking home one night in Soho. A ghostly figure swathed in white appeared to step out of the shadows. All the writer's glossy coiffure stood on end. He only regained his composure when he realised that it was a poster for the musical version of his most famous novel, *The Woman in White*.

*Silkie at the hairdressers*

*Silkie sees a phantom in the West End*

*Leo and Mewly Blue admire a portrait of the author*

# JAMES JOYCE

*I*N HIS FAMOUS novel *U-pussies*, his hero, Leo Blue, spends a day prowling around the alleys and dustbins of Dublin. After perusing the contents for discarded titbits he returns to his mate, the lovely Mewly Blue (not to be confused with Mewly Malone who steals a wheelbarrow [through streets broad and narrow] stacked with cockles and mussels).

*Dublin wasn't big enough for two Mewlies*

Cockles  Mussels

# *HENRY JAMS*

*H*ENRY JAMS WAS an American chef who marketed his own preserves such as 'Marmalade Cat Marmalade' and wrote a wonderful cookbook, *Portrait of a Lardy*. The innovative and literary recipes include: The Snails of Poynton, The Europe Peas, The Wings of a Dove, The Ham Bassadors, The Turn of the Corkscrew, The Golden Bowl and Daisy Miller-Lite.

*Henry and his prizewinning Jam*

*Henry in the kitchen*

# (HEEBY)
# G. B. SHAW

'*HEEBY-JEEBY*' WAS an exceptionally scary cat on account of his being so sharp and witty. His play *Pigmalion*, about a sow that was turned into a silk purse, did not work well as cat audiences are indifferent to the adventures of pigs unless they turn into sausages. However, adapted as a film (*My Fur Lady*) starring the exquisite Audrey Hep-purr, it was an instant success.

*Heeby Jeeby coaches his female lead in 'Pigmalion'*

*Heeby-Jeeby admires his creation*

*Cuteness personified – the girls and Marmee*

# LOUISA MAY ALCATT

*T*HIS SWEET-NATURED author wrote the darling *Little Women* about four lovely sisters. The story is set in the American civil war. They had a kind-hearted, gentle mother whom they called 'Marmee' (rhymes with Smarmee). Everyone who has read this charming book would have had a tear in their eye and would have occasionally felt slightly sick.

*The kind-hearted girls knitted for everyone in the town*

*Lord Georgie in his 'at home' outfit*

# GORGEOUS GEORGE, LORD BYRON

*U*NBEARABLY DASHING AND handsome, the world was in love with Byron – nobody more so than His Lordship himself. He adored himself in exotic outfits and was dining out in the Athens 'Parthenon Express' in a fetching Greek number (*see opposite*) when he fancied a game of marbles. He learned that Lord Elgin had taken them to London! 'What?' exclaimed His Swashbucklingness, 'I will snip him to pieces! I will tattoo a rude poem on his nose! I will return like a corsair in a storm! . . . retrieve the marbles or die!' Georgie whirled out in a flurry of fur, silk and steel and was not seen again.

*Georgie as a Corsair*

*Bossed-Well developing writer's cramp*

# DR SAMMY JOHNSON

Dr JOHNSON COMPILED a comprehensive dictionary of everything he enjoyed. Therefore, this book is a catalogue of food (sleep gets a mention). He transported his portly person along the length and breadth of Britain sampling Cornish pilchards, Dublin Bay prawns, Yarmouth bloaters . . . as far north as Orkney herring pâté. He was usually too sleepy or full to write any-thing down so his put-upon assistant, Bossed-Well, did the hard work.

Z z z

S
for
Stuffed

# GEORGES SIMENON

SIMENON CREATED INSPECTOR GOURMET, the rotund detective who glided smoothly from Mme Gourmet's home-cooked delights to the equally calorific pleasures of the *Brasserie Dauphine*. Occasionally, with a pilchard croissant in his pocket ('just in case') he slipped into police headquarters to check the staggering rise in crime figures. He finds (opposite) that a tiny snack of crustaceans ('brain food') helps him unravel the most fiendish of crimes.

*Gourmet lifts two suspects for attempting to be cute*

*Inspector Gourmet pauses for elevenses*

*Nick printing while Cesare plans supper*

# NICCOLÒ MACHIAVELLI

*H*IS MASTERPIECE IS *The Prints* written entirely with his own paws on a wet day. He wrote this for Lorenzo (the Magnificat) de'Medici in the hope that His Hugeness would invite him to the Palace for drinks and canapés, possibly a peacock dinner. However, Lorenzo recalled that Nick was a mate of Cesare Pawgia, the notorious poisoner, and would not allow the prolific scribbler within miles of his banqueting table. Disappointed, Machiavelli applied for the restaurant critic's job on the *Florence Evening Echo*. Not a chance.

*Lorenzo the Magnificat*

# FLUFFYKNEE DU MAURIER

THE YOUNG FLUFFYKNEE secured her enduring fame by writing *Rebecca*, a dark Cornish tale of murder, revenge, insecurity, pilchards, demented housekeepers, locked rooms, sprats, sunken boats, haughty insouciance, mackerel, clotted cream, dastardly deeds and other well-known Cornish fare. The hero is Max de Whisker who has a number of wives called Mrs de Whisker.

*The demented house-keeper, in the library, with the mackerel*

*The two Mrs De Whiskers eye each other up*

# CHARLES KITKINS

$K$ITKINS WOULD RATHER have pulled out all his whiskers than name a character 'Smith' or 'Jones'. Instead, he invented excruciatingly annoying names such as 'Nicholas Tickle-me', 'Martin Guzzle-It', 'Bob Scratchit', 'David Copperfurred', the sadistic 'Wackford Whisqueers' and the obsequious texter, 'u.r.a. Heep'. Readers would wait for new instalments to see how irritated they could be made by this cloying obsession.

THE GOLDEN LITTER

*Kitkins was hailed as a litter-tray genius*

*Cockney sparrows dropping hints*

# P. G. (PIGEON) WODEHOUSE

'*P*IGEON', NAMED AFTER his favourite dish, created the amiable upper-class twit, Bertie Whisker, and his resourceful valet, Jeeves. An expert on all things, Jeeves could particularly be relied upon in matters sartorial. As a result, Bertie was always turned out spiffingly. Occasionally he rebelled and tried to exit through the cat-flap wearing a garish T-shirt or unsuitable spats. This would give Jeeves a fit of the vapours more impenetrable than the steam baths in Istanbul.

*Bertie possessed a great number of bossy aunts*

*Bertie wears the wrong tie*

*Tabby inspired by his favourite food*

# TABBY BURNS

*T*HE SCOTTISH POET's most famous work is 'To a Mouse – Lightly Griddled'. This should have panicked the Scottish mouse population into hopping over Hadrian's Wall or catching the Irish ferry. However, as Burns pronounced it 'moose' – only moose and elks stampeded. And there was such a to-do at the Gretna Green Rotisserie where chef, Clawed-on Ramsay, fretted himself to a frazzle trying to grill a chocolate *mousse* without melting it.

*Mr Darcy is 'handbagged' by Frizzy*

# JANE PUSSTEN

JANE WROTE *Purred and Prejudice*, *Mansfield Puke*, *Purrsuasion*, *Northanger Tabby* and *Hiss and Hissability*. These are romantic novels with just a hint of bile. In *Purred and Prejudiced*, the heroine, Frizzy Bennet gives the haughty Mr Darcy the occasional belt round the ear or smack in the pedigree chops before settling down with him in his fine Palladian beanbag set in 200 acres of catnip.

*Mr Darcy's 'wet T-shirt'*
*moment in the TV version*

*Wise wizard: unwise hat*

# J. R. R. TOLKITTEN

TOLKITTEN INVENTED STRANGE furry and whiskery creatures called 'Hobbits'. Critics pointed out that they were nothing new – they all resembled Tolkitten himself – apart from 'Gandalf the Wizard' who looked like a borzoi in a hat, and 'Gollum' the subterranean creature, who resembled the hairless Mexican cat breed that usually comes 193rd in annual cat shows.

# BARONESS ORCZY

*T*HIS LADY'S FAMOUS creation was Sir Purrcy Blakeney, the Ginger Pimpernel – or as friends joked 'Pampered-Well'. During the French Revolution, Sir Purrcy, thought to be merely an over-dressed fop, smuggled doomed aristocratic mice out of Paris. Here he is at a society ball while actually hiding a refugee under his hat. Such tireless deceptions saved many a victim from the lethal mousetrap known as 'Madame Guillotine': a subject also covered in Dickens' *A Tale of Two Kitties.*

*Court ladies could also smuggle mouse refugees*

*Sir Purrcy with an asylum-seeker*

*Hairywatha at the catflap
of his tepee*

# HENRY LONG-HAIRED FELLOW

His poem: 'The Song of Hairywatha'

*By the shore of Itchy-Tummy*
*By the shining Big-Sea-Water*
*At the catflap of his wigwam,*
*In the pleasant summer, yawning,*
*Hairywatha stood and waited*
*All his fur was full of flea spray,*
*All his paws were neat and clean*
*And before him, in his saucer*
*Lots of jumping catfish gleam.*

*Hairywatha offers Minnehaha his*
*speciality: moth kebab*

*Hardy wishes he had stuck to poems*

# THOMOUSE HARDY

*T*HOMOUSE WAS A morose sort, writing West Country tales with deeply depressing endings. In *Tess of the D'Urbervilles* everything went paws-up for the heroine from the start. She became so monumentally annoyed with her creator's catalogue of doom-laden disasters that she changed her name to 'Hiss' and glared at Hardy from her portrait for the remainder of his gloomy career.

'Saddle I with a crap ending, would thee, Writer Hardy?' she hissed in perfectly accented Wessex dialect.

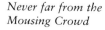

*Never far from the Mousing Crowd*

# JOHN KITS

THIS LONDON POET is, perhaps, most famous for his 'Ode to a Nightingale (on Toast)' – later, he was too busy to notice the anonymous publication of 'Return of the Nightingale' and 'Nightingale II'. It is interesting that Kits died suddenly in mysterious circumstances near the Spanish Steps in Rome close to the secret headquarters of 'Tweety Nostra' – the songbird mafia.

*A 'lurk' of nightingales*

Byron

Shelley

Ode
To a
Nightingale, Pome
(lightly toasted) Thrush
Take 1 nightingale (poached) When
Add parsley
Toast
Pepper
Salt

Rissoles

Ketchup

Kits has visitors

*Marcel the Deli-cat*

# MARCEL PURRST

*H*IS DOTING MOTHER saw Marcel as being 'delicate'; he, on the other hand, considered himself a 'deli cat'. His famous blockbuster *Remembrance of Tins Past* is really a catalogue of his favourite tinned delights; everything from canned clams to marinated mackerel, coddled cuttlefish to caviar. It was when he dipped a garlic *crouton* in a tin of *whelks Lyonnaise* that early memories flooded back to him. He died comparatively young, possibly because of a precariously-canned prawn.

*Life's tragedy: the sardine tin that won't open*

*Soldiers of the 49th Light Paw catch flying fishes*

# RUDYARD KITLING

Come you back to Mandalay
Where the old Chinchilla lay . . .
Can't you see his whiskers twitchin' from
Rangoon to Mandalay?
On the road to Mandalay
Where the flying fishes play
And the purring sounds like thunder outer
China 'cross the bay.

The Old Chinchilla on the
road to Mandalay

# THEODORE (THROUGH-THE-DOOR) DOSTOYEVSKY

*T*HEODORE WAS NICKNAMED 'Through-the-Door' because he was constantly catapulted outside for being annoyingly melodramatic. His books are peppered with snarlings, hissings, yodellings, fatal clawings, jealous spats,

histrionic howling, rug nibbling and poodle-baiting. Sparrows are beaten up, moths are menaced for hours, spiders are de-legged, cushions are disembowelled with the deadly back-leg-piston movement. Not the sort of cat you'd want on your sofa.

*Theo chucked out for over-dramatising in 'Cream and Punishment'*

*The Bruvvers Karamazov moth-bovvering in Moscow*

# AGATHA KITTY

**H**ER FAVOURITE CREATION was Her-Cute Poirot, a well-groomed and winsome Belgian detective whose 'little grey cells' prospered on a diet of *moules frites* and sugar mouse waffles. Ms Kitty's most famous invention, however, is *The Mouse Trap* which is still in position in the West End of London having trapped thousands of mice over more than fifty years.

*Agatha and her Miss Marple take tea and crumpets*

*Agatha and the Belgian detective*

# EDGAR ALLAN
## POO

BLACK AS A raven at midnight, Poo was never seen in day-
light. As darkness fell, he would rise from his beanbag in the
coal cellar and set about frightening the household witless.
His speciality was headless mice strategically placed in the
inky blackness, or worse, little surprises (as his name
suggests) for the unfortunate bare foot
to encounter. His 'how-to' book is
*The Fall of the House of Whisker.*

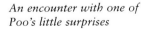

*An encounter with one of
Poo's little surprises*

*Poo on the Rue Morgue*

*Dorothy Wordsniff comes to the rescue*

# WILLIAM WORDSNIFF

*U*NFORTUNATELY, THIS FAMOUS Lakeland poet was a martyr to his hay fever:

> *I wandered lonely as a growl*
> *That snarls on high o'er vales and hills,*
> *When all at once I saw a crowd,*
> *Of pollen-ridden daffodils,*
> *Beside the lake, beneath the trees*
> *Well annoyed, I am one*
> *almighty sneeze.*

*Coleridge arrives with a gift*

# H. G. (ITCHY) WELLS

'ITCHY', WHO DETESTED any flea medication, took to writing science fiction to distract himself from scratching. His *War of the Wiles*, in which coyotes from Mars invade earth and frighten the daylights out of the road-runner population, was a great success, as was his *The Invisible Manx*: a tailless tabby became invisible and was thus able to raid all the larders in the land.

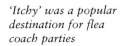

*'Itchy' was a popular destination for flea coach parties*

*The Invisible Manx (wearing false whiskers) stands behind Itchy*

# LEWHISS CARROLL

*L*EWHISS MISTOOK HIS own features in a mirror for those of a rival tomcat. A surreal snarling contest ensued, which, once the fur had settled, inspired the somewhat flaky author to write his masterpiece *A Hiss through the Looking Glass* featuring the rotund twins, Tweedletum and Tweedlepee and the Walrus and the Carpenter. Such pairings indicate the state of mind of a cat that could not recognise his own face.

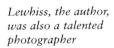

*Lewhiss, the author, was also a talented photographer*

*Lewhiss giving himself an awful fright*

*Bluie and Long Tom Silver*

# ROBERT 'BLUIE' STEVENSON

*I*T IS HARD TO imagine that this tiny scrap of a Blue Persian could write such adventurous novels as *Treasure Island* and *Catnipped*. Here is 'Bluie' languidly admiring the pirate and squid-napper, Long Tom Silver, with the treasure map, a clue to sand, sea and sardines. The buried casket, when opened, revealed a heart-stopping stash of canned fish taken from a Portuguese Cat O' War.

*Entertainment on 'Treasure Island'*

*Furlip Marlowe on the mean streets*

# RAYMOND CHANDLHAIR

CHANDLHAIR'S CREATION, Furlip Marlowe, has remained the epitome of the cool, laid-back private detective. Marlowe calmly snoozes his way through *The Big Sleep*, rising at midnight to lean languidly on a lamppost, light a Marlowboro, solve the crime and drift back to bed. In the film version, the actor, Humfurry Bogarte, played Marlowe in the same louche manner as that of his other detective role, Sam Spayed.

*Furlip's cool approach to crime solving*